Sarasa Woodblock Patterns

Design of flowers on red ground.
Carpet: material unknown; printed,
painted; mordant-dyed and wax-resist.
Used in Persia. 17th–18th century.

Sarasa Woodblock Patterns

Sachio Yoshioka
Supervising Editor

SHIKOSHA DESIGN LIBRARY

Stone Bridge Press · Berkeley, California

Published by
Stone Bridge Press
P.O. Box 8208
Berkeley, CA 94707
TEL 510-524-8732 • sbp@stonebridge.com • www.stonebridge.com

Book design by Fumio Shiozawa / cutcloud
http://cutcloud.net

Art direction by Art Books Shikosha Publishing Co., Ltd.

Woodblock images provided by The Yoshioka Collection.

Printed in China.

ISBN 978-1-933330-59-4

Sarasa Woodblock Patterns

Sarasa—also known as "chintz"—is cotton fabric dyed with decorative patterns. With madder (dark red) as its basic color, it developed in India over 2,000 years ago. Sarasa's vivid designs and high-quality cotton enabled it to spread throughout the world and become the progenitor of a wide variety of multicolored fabrics.

The earliest historical mention of sarasa appears in *Naturalis Historia* by Pliny the Elder (23–79). He mentions a type of patterned dyeing practiced in Egypt that is now thought to be sarasa, the technique for which was probably transmitted from India. Later, in the ruins of Fustat, the first capital city of Egypt under Arab rule, a fourteenth-century sarasa fragment was discovered that was imported, it is thought, from India.

It is difficult to dye cotton, which is made of natural fibers, in such colors as red and purple, which are natural dyes. This problem was overcome in India by using locally produced madder to create vibrant red colors.

From the sixteenth century onward, in the Age of Exploration, trade between East and West became increasingly frequent. And as Europe, China, and Japan came in contact with sarasa, this beautiful, vibrantly colored dyed fabric set off new waves of excitement.

There are three reasons for sarasa's powerful appeal. First is the material from which the fabric is made—cotton. Until the fifteenth century India was the principal producer of cotton, and it was therefore prized in northern countries for its softness, high retention of heat, and breathability. The second reason is that the fabric's colors resist fading when washed in water or exposed to sunlight. Third was the capability of the fabric to be dyed with two or three colors at the same time.

The Indian techniques developed into batik in Java, into copperplate printed cotton with finely detailed patterning in Europe, and finally into the basis for the principal means of printmaking today, silkscreen, which strongly impacted the work of the Oberkampf factory at Jouy in France and William Morris's workshop (Liberty Print) in England.

There are two main methods for producing sarasa—hand-painted and woodblock-printed. The patterns produced by these two techniques are multifarious, following the technological variations employed in different countries.

There are two types of woodblock dyeing. One involves using a fixative, the other a wax. When a fixative is used, the dye adheres to the area where the fixative has been applied. When a wax is used, the area to which the wax has been applied resists the dye, leaving that area white. Depending on the design, as many as ten blocks might be used on one piece of cloth to achieve the desired effect.

This book introduces genuine woodblocks such as those used principally by craftsmen in India, but also in Persia and elsewhere, where patterns were engraved in hard, durable teak.

Against the canvas provided by cotton fabrics, birds swoop through the air, animals frolic, stylized flowers and plants burst forth in a celebration of life. The Indian gods and the Indian people mingle together. Gorgeous geometrical patterns and sumptuous spirally scrollwork weave their magic. These wonderful patterns, it is hoped, can be preserved for our own times so that we can once again experience the beautiful stylizations of their art.

How to Use This Book

The images in this book can be appreciated as they are for their intrinsic beauty. Or, if you are so inclined, you can reproduce and use them in your art or graphic design projects.

All of the images in this book can be used royalty free. They can be downloaded from the Shikosha Design Library website, which is linked to www.stonebridge.com. Many of the images are available for free download at lower resolutions for hobbyists and home users. High-resolution, high-quality versions that are intended for graphic arts professionals can be downloaded from the site for a nominal fee. Once you copy or download an image, you can use your own design tools and software to edit and manipulate it to suit your needs.

For Hobbyists and Home Users

You do not need fancy tools or software to capture or use the images in this book.

- Take this book to any photocopy service bureau and ask them to copy an image and enlarge or reduce it, in black and white or in color.
- Use tracing paper to capture outlines of images or parts of images that you can then fill in and recolor to your liking.
- If you have a decent close-up lens on your camera, take photographs and reprint them as often as you like; this works even better if you have a digital camera hooked up to an inexpensive inkjet printer at home.
- If you are artistically inclined yourself, you can freely redraw the images, using them for inspiration as you explore your own themes and develop your own designs.

For Graphic Arts Professionals

If you are a graphic arts professional you are probably familiar with using computer software to manipulate, re-color, resize, crop, and otherwise transform both line art and grayscale or color images. Here we introduce three basic techniques using Adobe Photoshop CS—solarization, adding color to black and white images, and changing image color. Photoshop is not the only software that offers these tools, and of course there are many other ways that you can use downloaded images to achieve your ends.

Throughout this book, cmyk values are given adjacent to images for reference. You can of course change these color values as desired, or use them to create matching or complementary colors. Running heads throughout indicate the types of effects displayed, including solarization and colorization and colorized solarization. The effect is usually accompanied by the original image or artwork, with the original sometimes smaller or larger than the effect depending on visual interest.

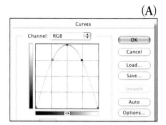
(A)

SOLARIZATION

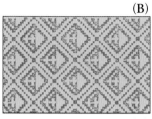
(B)

Solarization is one type of effect you can apply to photos. In general, solarization results when you purposely overexpose film as it's developing to invert the brightness or color of one part or all of a photo. Solarization uniquely gives the sense of subtly stacking film positives and negatives on top of one another. Here, we'll use a tone curve to recreate this effect, then freely alter the image even more.

(C)

First, open the original image. Then use the Curves function to adjust the image's tones. Make a curve like that in (A), and the original image will change as shown in (B), displaying the solarization effect. The steeper you make the angle of the curve line, the more intense the solarization will become. Conversely, the gentler the curve line, the gentler the solarization. See (C).

(D)

By using the Curves panel to set tones, you'll be able to play with the look and feel more effectively than you would using the Solarization filter alone. By selecting the Freehand button on the Curves panel and experimenting with various values, you can create an even greater variety of solarization effects. See (D, E).

(E)

ADDING COLOR TO BLACK AND WHITE IMAGES

To precisely color in an outline, use the method below:

1. Connect and close any segments whose lines or borders are incomplete.
Use a drawing tool or, if you have one, a pen tablet. Examine the image carefully. If there are broken lines around the areas you want to color in separately from the background, draw a line or lines to extend them to the margins or to connect and

Examples of solarization.

close them. You do this so that when you click on an area with the Magic Wand tool the selection does not extend to where it is not wanted. This job can be rather time-consuming depending on the original image.

2. Make a separate layer for the outlines only.

Select only the lines around the areas to be colored in. Copy this selection onto a new layer (the "line" layer). (You can make the result cleaner using the Level Correction or Defringe functions.)

3. Make a layer for coloring.

In the line layer select the transparent, non-line areas. Copy this selection into a new layer (the "coloring layer") beneath the line layer. Use the Fill function to color the selection white. (If you enlarge the selection slightly before filling, you won't leave any area uncolored.)

4. Color freely.

In the coloring layer, activate Lock Transparent Pixels. Use the Magic Wand tool, the Paint Bucket tool, or any of the brushes to apply color to the image any way you like.

Create additional variations by changing the color of the image outlines. If you lock transparency when coloring, the color won't go outside the lines, and your image will have a clean look.

CHANGING COLORS IN AN IMAGE

There are many ways to change colors, but here is the most basic. Open the original image. In the Adjustments menu select Hue/Saturation. Move any of the sliders to change the color.

To change only part of the image, first select the area you wish to change, then adjust the color using the sliders.

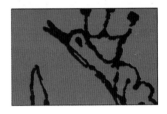

Adding color to black and white images.

Changing color in an image as a result of moving the Adjustments sliders.

Examples of the types of projects that can be made using the designs and patterns in this book.

Applications

There is no limit to what you can do with the images and designs in this book. You may, for example, just use a small piece of a design as a part of a logo or an understated decorative motif on a greeting card. Or you can take an entire design and expand it into a wall-size mural to decorate a hallway or bathroom or ceiling.

The designers of this book have intentionally taken the original artworks and manipulated them in various ways to demonstrate the possibilities and especially the surprising results when colors and images are flipped, tiled, or otherwise manipulated. What began as a fairly standard Asian representational motif now becomes a thoroughly modern and almost abstract rendering that still suggests an Asian aesthetic but is now charged with a modern sensibility. The color changes and manipulations in this book are just examples. If you download the images yourself, you will be able to explore many more possibilities than can possibly be shown here.

PROJECT IDEAS

Below are some possible uses for the images in this book.

- Fine artworks
- Stencils and rubber stamps
- Menus
- Web page graphics
- Posters
- Tattoos and henna body painting
- Bookplate designs
- Architectural and sculptural elements
- Picture frames
- Collages
- Greeting cards
- Fabric designs
- Lampshades
- Signs
- Quilts, embroidery, and beading
- Scrapbooks
- Cell-phone covers
- Mosaics and tilework
- Cake decorations
- Logos and letterheads

LOGOS AND LETTERHEADS

Printing on different shades of paper will produce different effects. Try using textured paper like Japanese *washi* in your inkjet printer to create antiqued designs with subtle surface qualities. Such prints are often suitable for framing on their own and can be an inexpensive and stylish way to decorate your personal space.

| Original Sarasa Fabric

C : 50
M : 50

Original Woodblock with Solarization, Colorized Solarization, and Colorization

C : 60
M : 80
Y : 80
K : 70

C : 30
M : 60
Y : 90

M : 30
Y : 100

C : 10
M : 100

Original Woodblock with Colorization; Textile Detail

M : 100
Y : 30

C : 100
Y : 100

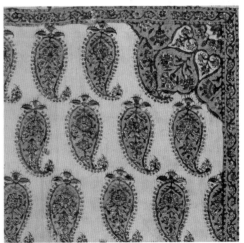

Original Woodblock with Colorization; Textile Detail | 19

C : 100
Y : 70

C : 70
Y : 100

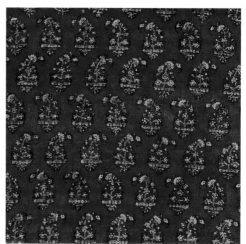

Original Woodblock with Colorization; Textile Detail

C : 70
M : 100

C : 100
Y : 30

Original Woodblock with Colorization; Textile Detail | 21

M : 100
Y : 100

| Original Woodblock with Solarization, Colorized Solarization, and Colorization

M : 50

C : 50
M : 40
Y : 100

K : 100

C : 20
M : 10
Y : 100

Original Woodblock with Colorization; Textile Detail

C : 70
M : 100
Y : 20

C : 100
Y : 50

Original Woodblock with Colorization; Textile Detail | 25

M : 100
Y : 80
K : 50

C : 60
M : 40
Y : 40

| Original Woodblock with Colorization; Textile Detail

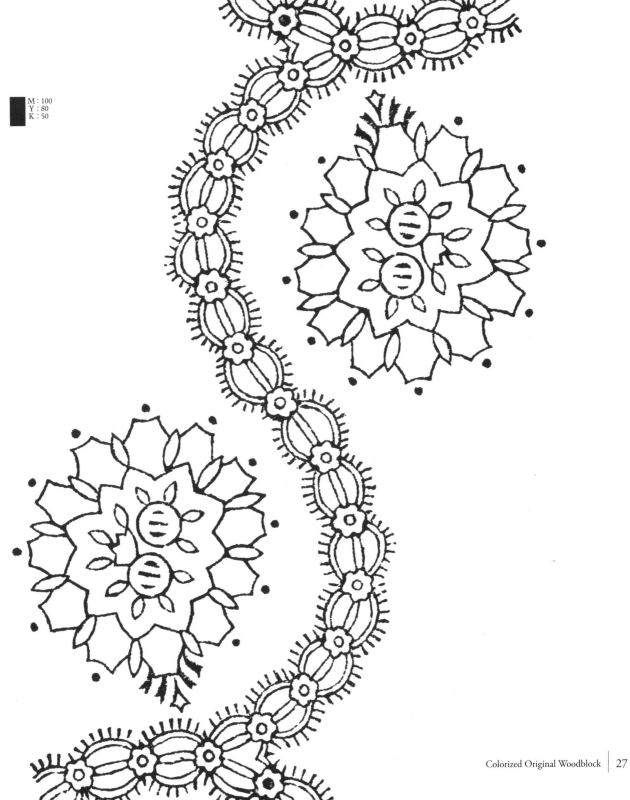

M : 100
Y : 80
K : 50

C : 40
Y : 100

| Original Woodblock with Solarization, Colorized Solarization, and Colorization

M : 100
Y : 20

C : 30
M : 70
Y : 70
K : 70

| Original Woodblock

M : 60

C : 100
M : 50
Y : 10
K : 50

C : 80
M : 80
Y : 5

Y : 70

 | Original Woodblock with Solarization and Colorization

C : 40
M : 70
Y : 50
K : 30

C : 50
Y : 30

Original Woodblock with Solarization and Colorization | 35

■	C : 80
	M : 80
	Y : 90
	K : 10
▨	C : 50
	Y : 10

Original Woodblock with Solarization and Colorization

C : 50
K : 100

C : 50
Y : 50

Original Woodblock with Solarization and Colorization | 37

Original Woodblock; Textile Detail | 39

40 | Original Woodblock; Textile Detail

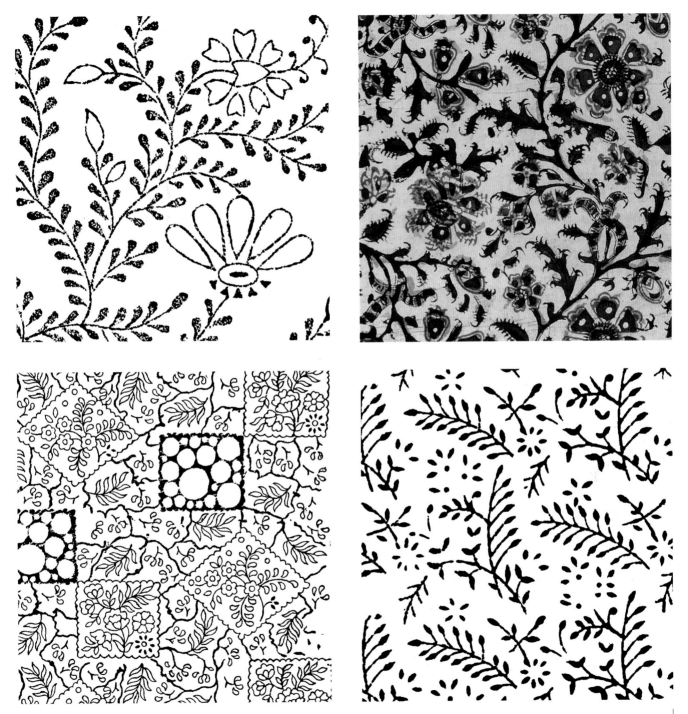

| Original Woodblock

| Colorization of Facing-Page Woodblock

C : 100
M : 70
Y : 100

M : 90
Y : 100

C : 100
M : 100

Original Woodblock with Solarization and Colorized Solarization | 45

C : 80
M : 80
Y : 30

M : 20
Y : 50

C : 70
M : 90
Y : 40

M : 50
Y : 40

Original Woodblock with Colorization; Textile Detail | 49

C : 60
M : 100
Y : 90

C : 40
M : 10
Y : 80

Original Woodblock with Colorization; Textile Detail

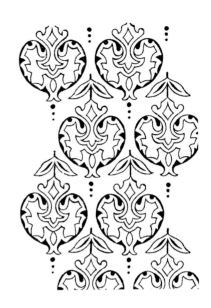

C : 100
M : 70
Y : 40

C : 60
M : 30
Y : 30

C : 60
M : 100
Y : 70

C : 70
M : 40
Y : 10

| Original Woodblock with Colorization

C : 10
M : 90
Y : 100

C : 20
M : 40
Y : 80

Original Woodblock with Colorization; Textile Detail | 53

C : 100
M : 90
Y : 90

C : 40
M : 10
Y : 90

C : 10
M : 90
Y : 100

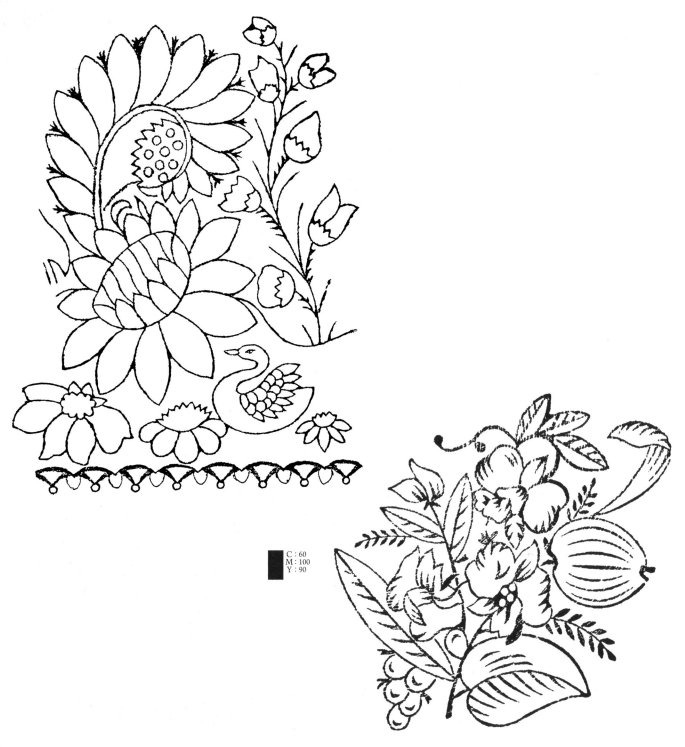

C : 60
M : 100
Y : 90

C : 80
M : 30
Y : 60

C : 10
M : 60
Y : 20

C : 90
M : 40
Y : 30

C : 50
M : 50
Y : 60

| Original Woodblock with Colorization

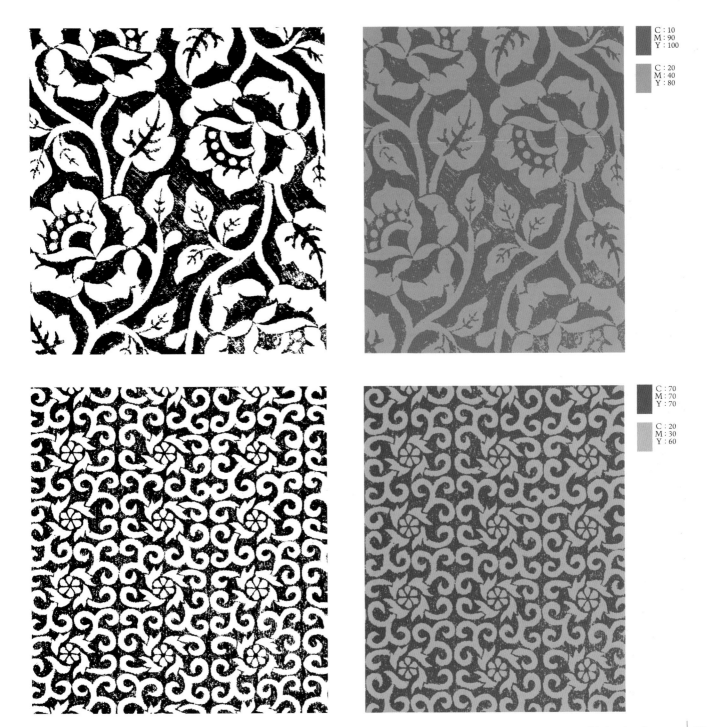

C : 10
M : 90
Y : 100

C : 20
M : 40
Y : 80

C : 70
M : 70
Y : 70

C : 20
M : 30
Y : 60

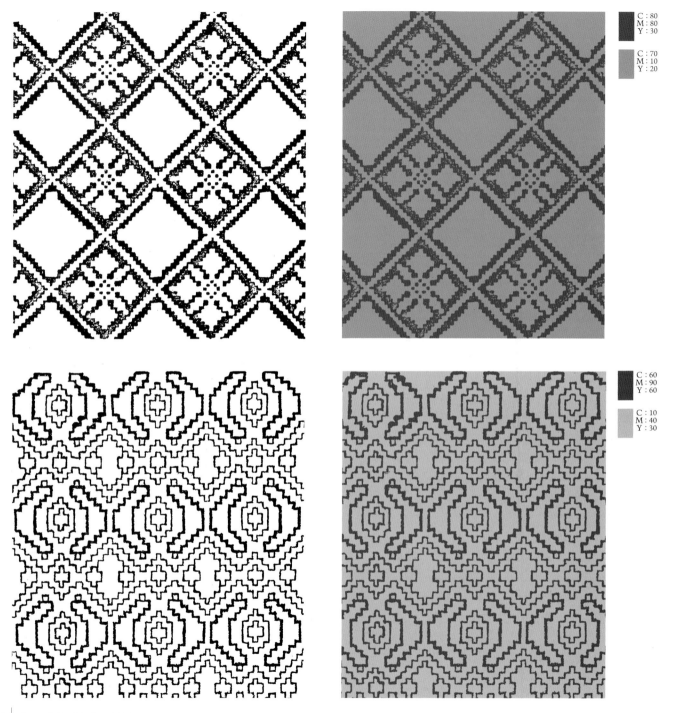

C : 80
M : 80
Y : 30

C : 70
M : 10
Y : 20

C : 60
M : 90
Y : 60

C : 10
M : 40
Y : 30

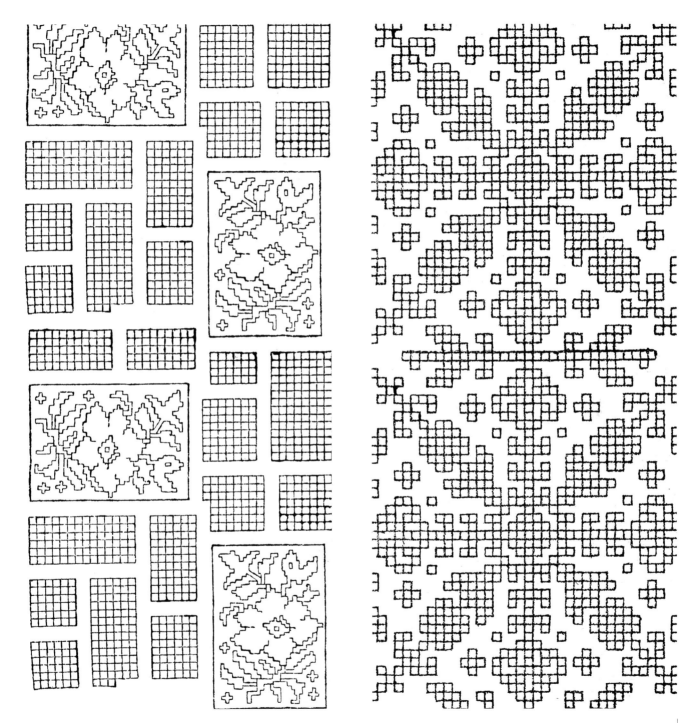

C : 80 M : 70 Y : 20	Y : 70
M : 50 Y : 30	C : 100 M : 45 Y : 40

| Original Woodblock with Colorization

C : 80
M : 80
Y : 40

C : 60
M : 20
Y : 40

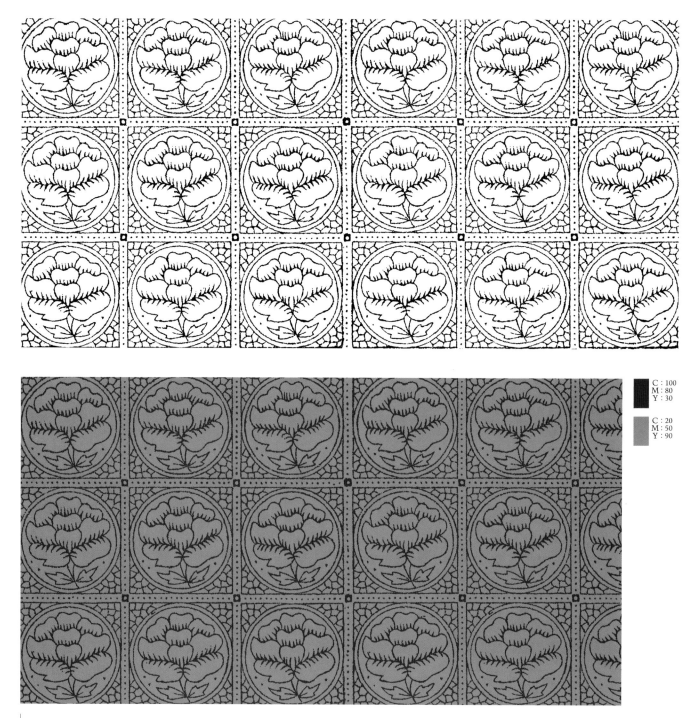

C : 100
M : 80
Y : 30

C : 20
M : 50
Y : 90

| Original Woodblock with Colorization

C : 10
M : 90
Y : 100
K :

C : 60
Y : 20

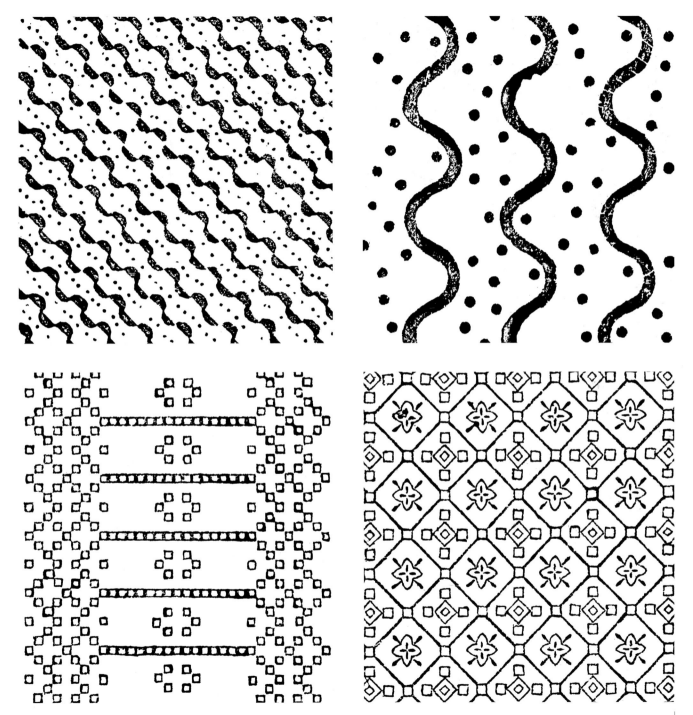

C : 60
M : 100
Y : 90

C : 60
M : 10
Y : 20

| Original Woodblock with Solarization and Colorization

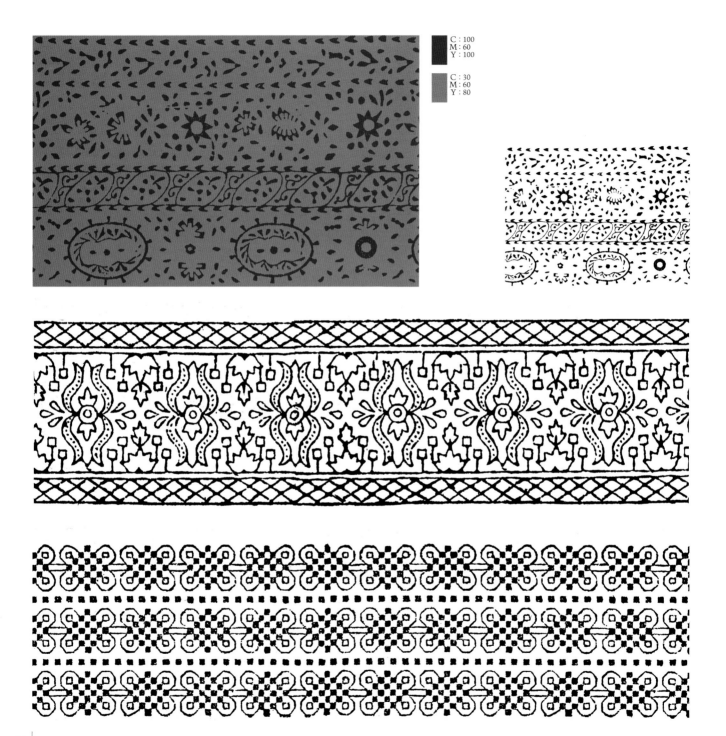

C : 100
M : 60
Y : 100

C : 30
M : 60
Y : 80

C : 80
M : 90
Y : 50

C : 20
M : 30
Y : 80

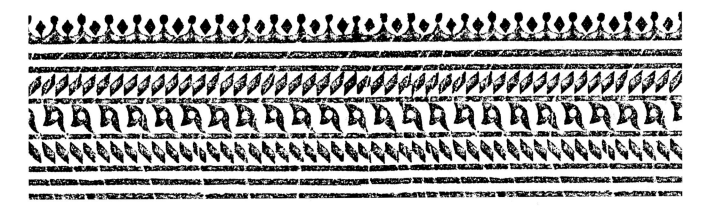

C : 90
M : 40
Y : 90
K : 20

C : 50
M : 50
Y : 10

C : 80
M : 60
Y : 90

C : 30
M : 60
Y : 60

C : 100
M : 80
Y : 20

C : 50
M : 80
Y : 90

Original Woodblock with Solarization and Colorization

C : 70
M : 40
Y : 50

C : 10
M : 50
Y : 40

C : 70
M : 50
Y : 80

C : 10
M : 20
Y : 40

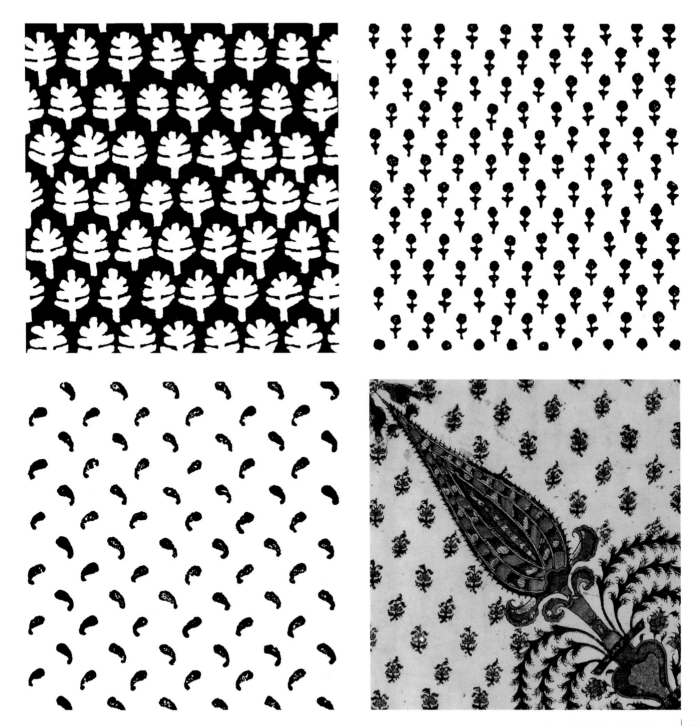

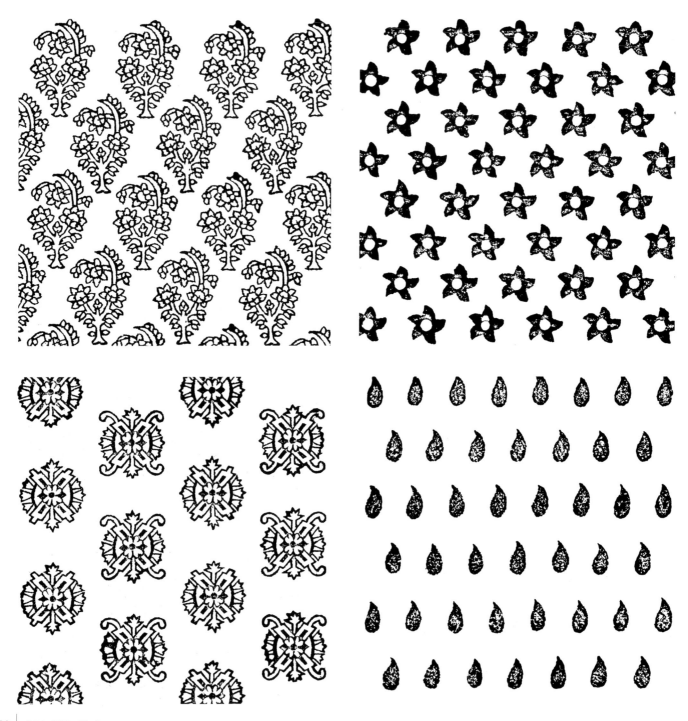

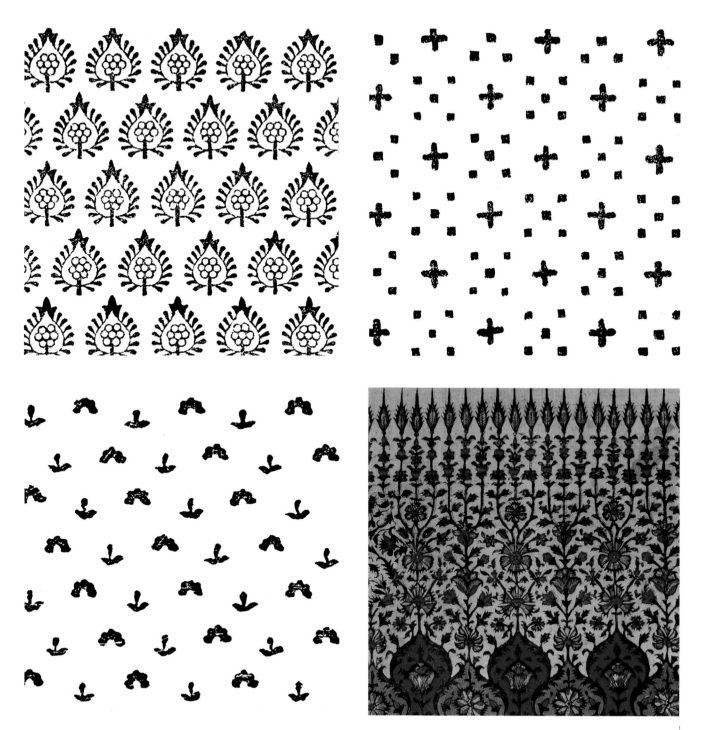

Original Woodblock; Textile Detail | 93

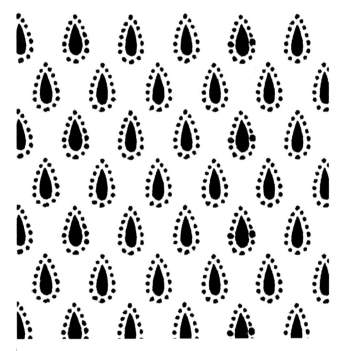

Original Woodblock; Textile Detail

C : 80
M : 70
Y : 100

M : 70
Y : 40

C : 80
M : 80
Y : 50

C : 80
M : 20
Y : 40

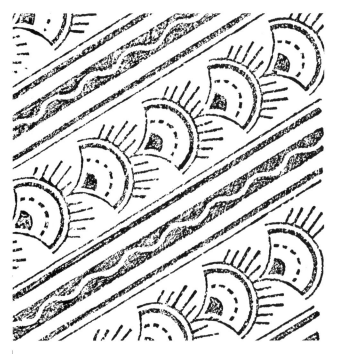
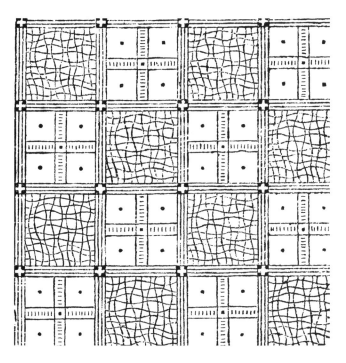

98 | Original Woodblock; Textile Detail

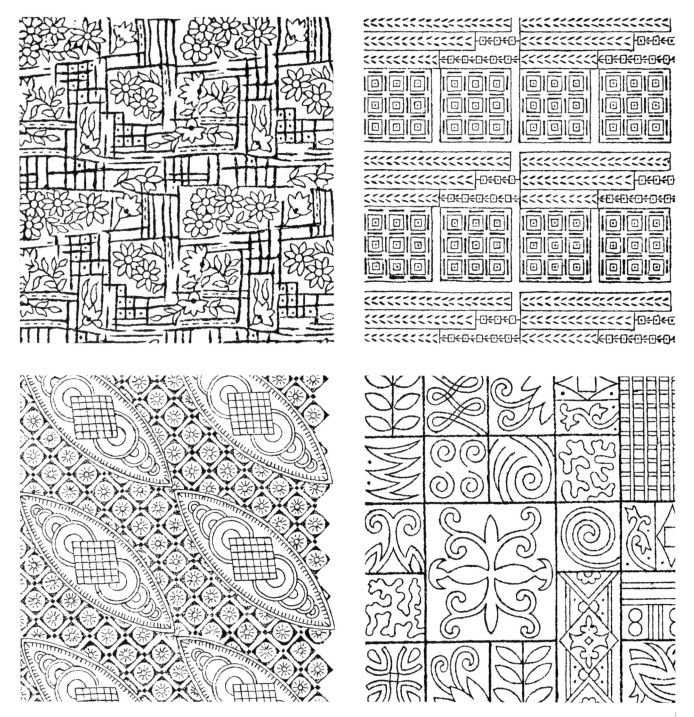

C : 50
M : 100
Y : 100

M : 70
Y : 90

M : 30
Y : 80

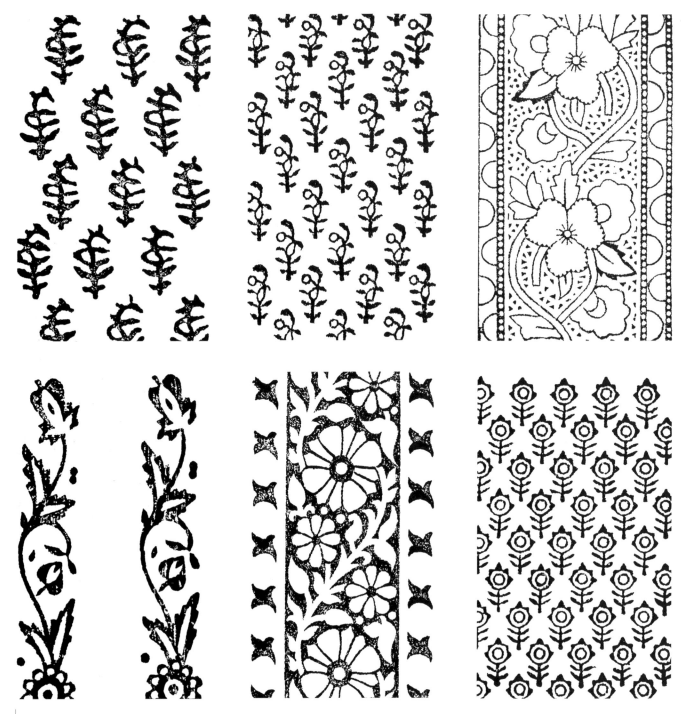

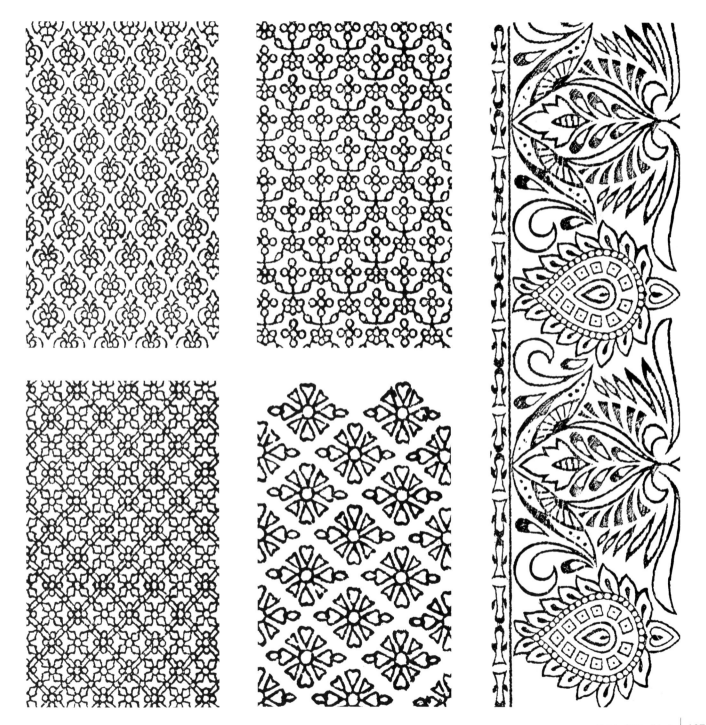

| Original Woodblock with Colorization

M : 90
Y : 70

C : 10
M : 20
Y : 20

M : 100
Y : 100

C : 80
M : 90
Y : 20

M : 50
Y : 70

M : 100
Y : 100

C : 50
K : 100

M : 100
Y : 80

Original Woodblock with Colorization

C : 100
M : 70

C : 50
M : 90
Y : 30

M : 100
Y : 100

Original Woodblock with Colorization and Colorized Woodblock | 115

Original Woodblock with Colorization and Colorized Woodblock

C : 70
M : 100

C : 40
M : 30
Y : 20

Original Woodblock with Colorization | 117

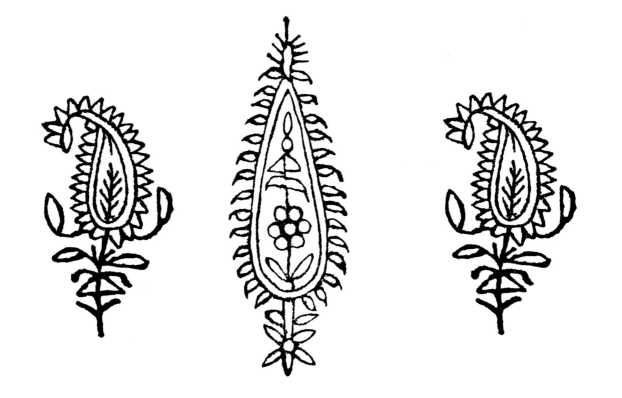

M : 100
Y : 100